What Others ar[...]
The Explosion Takes Both Legs

"As meditations on war, these poems are revelation. Soulful, hell-bent, fearless, riddled with pathos and hard-won psychological truth. While Stevens draws upon his combat experience in Iraq for source material, what illuminates these poems are his abiding humanity and his preoccupation with the mysteries of the human heart. True war stories, but make it poetry."

—Gabe Hudson, author of *Dear Mr. President*

❖ ❖ ❖

"J.B. Stevens' writing is a unique fusion of war poetry, pulp fiction, and pop culture references. Sometimes, he's a red-star cluster warning of danger. Other times, he's an artillery-delivered illumination round. Regardless, his work is stunningly insightful and explosively entertaining. Read on for some mental fireworks, delivered on-time and on-target!"

—Randy Brown,
author of *Welcome to FOB Haiku: War Poems from Inside the Wire*
and *So Frag & So Bold: Short Poems, Aphorisms & Other Wartime Fun*

❖ ❖ ❖

"War as close-calls, confusion and waste. These poems keep coming at you, relentlessly, like one punch after another. Collectively, they will leave you reeling."

—Bill McCloud,
author of *The Smell of the Light: Vietnam, 1968-1969*

❖ ❖ ❖

"Stevens' poetry is like watching old school fight clips on YouTube all night long. Like binge watching 'Diners, Drive-Ins, and Dives' with your crush under the stars. It's going home after a long day of work and blasting Nirvana through your stereo. It's making the perfect s'mores after finally getting the campfire going. Which is to say, J.B. Stevens' *The Explosion Takes Both Legs* is a haymaker straight to the heart, and it's beautiful."

—Shawn Berman, author of *Mr. Funnyman*
and editor of *The Daily Drunk*

❖ ❖ ❖

"'They are gone, and I hope it didn't hurt.' Through his honest and direct depictions of death, survivor's guilt, and the alluring simplicity of war, J.B. Stevens documents how to be a veteran is to forever miss a part of yourself still out on the unfinished patrol. You don't laugh in the face of death because you want to die, you laugh because it's the best way to go. Haunting and visceral images that stick with you long after reading."

—Zakariah Johnson,
author of *Mink: Skinning Time in Wisconsin*
and *Egg on Her Face: Stories of Crime, Horror, and the Space in Between*

The Explosion Takes Both Legs

Noir Poems
from the
War in Iraq

J.B. Stevens

Middle West Press LLC
Johnston, Iowa

❖ ❖ ❖

Poetry / Iraq War / Military Life

*The Explosion Takes Both Legs:
Noir Poems from the War in Iraq*
by J.B. Stevens

ISBN (print): 978-1-953665-20-1
ISBN (e-book): 978-1-953665-21-8
Library of Congress Control Number: 2023937530

❖ ❖ ❖

Middle West Press LLC
P.O. Box 1153
Johnston, Iowa 50131-9420
www.middlewestpress.com

❖ ❖ ❖

*Special thanks to James Burns of Colorado Springs, Colorado
and Nathan Didier of Cedar Falls, Iowa!*

Your patronage helps publish great military-themed writing!
www.aimingcircle.com

To Erica & Claire

CONTENTS

This is My Rifle

War War War War War War

War War War War War War The enormity of it all explodes, a crushing 1776-pound red boulder...
War War War War War
War War War War War War I didn't foresee the Arabian poets coming for my scalp—I should've.
War War War War War
War War War War War War Smashing down in my chest and there is no nuance today or in life ...
War War War War War
War War War War War War My chest is open and my heart out and is the world's now, I accept.
War War War War War
War War War War War War The waves of shit roll over me and I didn't ask for any of it but here ...

The taking begins—I knew it was coming but didn't see the direction and for that I've been blindsided.

My response and you hate me and I wanted to be truth and I wanted to be joy and nothing mattered ...

I wrap-up in green and blue and white and red. So much red. Make it red & dripping & you get an MFA.

J.B. STEVENS

Fat Cook Gunfight

I once got in a gunfight,
On the edge of Sadr City,
With a fat cook standing by my side.

I was young and immortal,
In a beige world,
Of sadness,
The fat cook told me to go fuck myself.

I made him truck hot chow to my combat outpost for my men.

Mine.

Fat cook loathed me for it.
But I didn't care and never will.
Fuck fat cook.

It smelled of dry concrete, and dust got in my mouth,
And the sounds left my ears and it was peaceful and bright.
And the sun cut through the grime and it is shining in my memory.

Fat cook was a Sergeant and I was a Captain,
And Heartbreak Ridge was my fully funded MFA program.
The next day cook asked me to put him in for an award,
And I did,
And he got it,
And I will live forever,
And I will never die.

I can never die.

This French 75 is a Living Thing

It rests in my Champagne flute,
And the bubbles live,
They tickle my nose,
They tell me I endure,
I exist.

And this French 75 calls me,
This one,
Like the last four,
In this dive bar,
In this dive city,
In this dive life.

The kick is real,
I drink until reality stops being so fucking real.

One ounce of gin,
And a half ounce of lemon juice,
Fresh squeezed,
Two dashes of simple syrup,
Shaken until chilled.
Strained and topped with two ounces of Champagne,
Garnished with a lemon twist.

And I drink the magical elixir until the welcome peace soaks me,
MacElhone prepared it in Harry's Bar,
MacElhone named it after the shell,
Kill the Germans,
The French 75 kills the memory.

Those Doughboys call upon me,
Late—when my eyes are closed,
And the dust comes.

J.B. STEVENS

Iraqi sand grinding the web of my toes,
I drink 75s until the grit leaves.

We are connected,
And they drank these in Harry's Bar,
And I am tied to them,
And it hurts,
And tears fall into a Champagne flute,
And the bubbles live,
And the welcome peace soaks me.

And I drink until it kills the memories.
I smell the lemon twist.
The welcome peace soaks me.

Metric

Georgia is made of inches and feet and yards,
These are important units of measurement—
In the South.

And football is a war game that feels like more (in Georgia and Alabama
and Texas) when you are young and innocent and free.
10 yards for a first down—I learned that before I can recall,
Before I could walk,
And yards are my childhood,
And yards are my innocence.

The M4 rifle—produced by Colt in Hartford, Connecticut—
fires a 5.56-millimeter round,
That was the first metric measurement we learned,
Or cared about.

When calling for artillery fire,
(Steel death from a distance.)
We learned meters.

In 2004 I discovered 64 paces (for me) was 100 meters,
I can still feel meters in my marrow,
And a kilometer is 1,000 meters,
Metric is clearer than the English Standard,
Preferable when summoning death,
From a distance.

Precision is critical,
To not kill yourself or your platoon,
When you are a 24-four-year-old Lieutenant and scared and
your fire support Sergeant is a piece of shit,
You must only kill the other ones,
Not yourself,

Or your platoon.
(Even if you would be fine with yourself.)
Only the other ones.

The first time I called for fire was at a palm grove near Iskandariya—
South of Baghdad,
In 2007.
I don't remember how many meters it was,
Or how many people died,
But it was a largish number.
(For both.)

Metric is clearer for these kinds of things,
More efficient,
And now I know the metric system,
But only for distance and width,
It is clearer,
And more efficient.

As I Clean My Rifle

The quiet holds me,
And the flow state hits.
I could do this in my sleep,
Zen through rifle disassembly.
A blindfold party trick that no one cares about.

The warm embrace of C.L.P.,
(Cleans, Lubricates, and Protects—a wondrous product.)
The smell knocks and I spit out the taste of Arabian sand.
And I.E.D. aftershocks rattle in my chest,
And the dry heat comes and the never-ending exhaustion,
I'm still tired from that last patrol,
And always will be—a problem that no one cares about.
The last patrol.

I loved my M4,
And I love my AR15. Mine.
Ecstasy through assembly.

I worship at the altar of Eugene Stoner—
Stoner's gift was blessed,
And I am forever thankful.

Nirvana through a trigger-pull.
Clarity through taking souls.
Enlightenment through stacking bodies.

An existence no one cares about.

J.B. STEVENS

Never Ask

The Sergeant was always well-lotioned,
His dark skin sparkled, wrinkle free,
And if we had Botox back then I'd be suspicious,
    but we did not—did we?

We spent our days preparing for war,
And our nights dreaming of glory,
And his moustache was perfect.

He always invited the young privates to stay at his house,
And many did.
The barracks is not a happy place.

But I never asked,
And he never told,
And that was a stupid policy.

But the Infantry is a rough place,
For rough men,
Trying to prove something to someone,
Usually their father and themselves.

He kept up his lotion,
And his well-trimmed mustache,
And I never asked.

Incoming Fire from a New Transport Platoon

The first mission outside the wire is frightening,
I remember mine in sepia and with a Metallica soundtrack and
a firework smell and a bitter taste.

The sun is over-bright,
And the world is loud,
And your senses are pegged,
Your adrenaline dumps.
And your heart is going to erupt from your chest in a bloody
and meaty blossom.

The days drag,
And the blacktop goes on forever,
And the potholes and dead animal carcasses,
And trash piles and new asphalt,
Are all spots where the improvised explosive devices live.
And the story never ends.

The complacency sets in,
And you accept that there is no reason,
And what happens happens,
And you stop caring,
And just do your best to not die,
Because it would make your mom sad,
Not because you give a shit.

It came for me after thirteen months,
W's surge fucked me,
And no one remembers.
And I was long-past caring,
And I was south of Baghdad.

A new transport platoon rolled through my space,
They were still over-bright and loud and pegged,
Not yet going on forever.
Their road still had an end.

They started shooting at me,
With American guns,
They were scared,
But it was my space,
And that day I'd borrowed a tank.

Ping-Ping-Ping,
Friendly fire ringing my doorbell.

I got on the radio,
Stop fucking shooting at me,
Or I will shoot back,
And I'm much-fucking-better at it.
And I have a tank.

The doorbell stopped ringing.
They said sorry,
And I accepted their apology,
And they got to the end.

The Combat Infantryman (person) Badge

In 1941, during the start of World War Two, no one wanted
to join the American Infantry.
As an Infantryman (now person) you get shot at, a lot,
And you shoot back, a lot,
And killing is the name of the game,
Close with and destroy the enemy through fire and maneuver.
Fuck you, die for your country,
I'm not dying for mine.
You first.
Fuck you.

To get more Soldiers to assume this noble and necessary load,
The War Department (better name than Defense Department) created
a new award,
The Combat Infantryman's Badge,
The C.I.B.
The Mark of a Man (now person).

The CIB said you'd been in the shit and you are still here,
Or something.

Morale increased,
And men joined (now people),
And I got mine in 2007,
And if you ask nicely—I will show you the picture.
(The photo is bloody—but I was young and men (now people) heal
quickly when they are young.)

It is blue and has a wreath,
I have mine mounted in a shadow box,
Next to my Great Grandpa's (One of the original's)
One day I will give it to my daughter.

And war is so fucking stupid.

Pace Counts

Losing Legs

The Combat Infantryman (person) Badge was a huge hit,
It made the grunts,
The meat ground to burger,
Elite.

So successful,
Big Green decided to keep the party going,
It gets hard to recruit when there is two decades of pointless war,
The fiesta can't stop.

The Combat Action Badge was 1941's after-party,
The 2005 redux.

It is for everyone,
An equal opportunity shit-show.

In 2008 there was a female lawyer,
Captain,
Who wanted her party.
Her meaty cotillion.

The Battalion Commander let her go on a patrol with my buddy,
And an E.F.P. (Explosively Formed Penetrator or Projectile depending on your intelligence officer and the timeframe you served, both are correct [really] but military-types love to argue about nomenclature and prove other people wrong it is an ego/alpha-dog type thing, I don't enjoy that so here we are) popped to her right.

A laser beam of molten copper took her legs,
I remember the smell,
The taste.

(Not Tammy Duckworth)

And now she has two stumps.
And a Juris Doctorate.
And a C.A.B.

The Iraqi Female Suicide Bomber Who Blew-Off Her Arms and Legs

The smell of burnt meat came through the photos,
It tickled the back of my brain,
Burnt meat smells different (better) than burnt hair,
I didn't know you can smell photos,
But you can.

I learned a hard fact—
When you utilize a suicide-bombing vest,
Make sure the maker knows what the fuck they are doing,
Professional work is important in all things,
Even terrorism.

The woman was a victim,
We know that,
But I was glad I wasn't there when she pushed the button.

She was probably a widow,
Probably overcome with grief and rage and confusion,
I still don't know why I was there,
She belonged.

I didn't.
I still don't.
I don't belong anywhere and I know that,
Forever-War is very confusing.

The maker under-powered the suicide-vest/bomb,
When the woman pushed the button,
It sounded like a firework,
And it blew off her arms and legs,
And lower face,

But—

It didn't kill anyone other than her,
And she died slow.
And she died hurting.

You really need a professional for these things.
Professionalism matters.

The Iraqi Disabled-Kid Suicide-Bomb Squad

They told us it was a school for disabled kids,
The translator used the hard-R-word,
I might have said it, but I won't,
But I don't think that is right now.
I didn't always know these things.

The school's belly was empty.

We asked a neighbor where the kids were,
And our translator said the neighbor said terrorists took them,
And strapped bombs to their chest,
And sent them into the crowds,
No one looked twice at disabled kids.

I don't know if it is true.

I don't know if anything is true.

The next week, numerous markets got hit with suicide bombs,
Borne by children.

I don't know Islam's stance on the issue,
But I hope the kids are all right,
In their next existence.
Virgins and such—if that's the goal,
(That part seems to float a bit.)

But I don't know if ever really happened,
Or if it was all some dusty memory,
Shoved into my mind,
From too many stories,
And too much sadness.

And no sleep.

J.B. STEVENS

Juba the Sniper

Juba killed at least 37 Americans,
But no one is sure.

Maybe some CIA paper-pusher somewhere knows the truth,
But it is buried in a file.

Maybe the true-truth is on WikiLeaks,
All my worst true-truths are on WikiLeaks.

I saw somewhere he'd killed 600,
That seams unreasonable,
Maybe.
Maybe it was a dream, and this is as well.

Juba is the myth,
The boogeyman,
Keep your head down,
Even in the dream.

Do the right thing.

I still don't know if he is true-truth,
Or if he is my own Dread Pirate Roberts,

Sometimes at night,
When it is dark,
And the dream-truth comes,

I think of Juba.

Fuck you, Juba.

You missed.

A Ghost in an Arabian Desert

After we returned,
We had a ceremony and the commander said many nice things,
I got a Bronze Star.

My mother and father and brothers met me at the base,
Because my fiancée had cheated and left,
And my brother brought me ice-cream.

My fire-support officer,
3-0,
He was alone as well,
Because women want a man that exists,
Not a ghost in an Arabian desert,
In limbo at some forgotten combat outpost,
With no phone or email,
Praying to not get blown to fuck.

But not caring too much,
Because the after seems far more peaceful.

3-0 and I went to Prague,
To chase wine and women and wonder,
But I couldn't sleep,
And the night terrors woke me,
They woke him too,
And I screamed in the corner,
But he didn't talk about it and acted as if it never happened,
And that is kind of him.

And Prague is beautiful.

And I don't know if I am a ghost in an Arabian desert,
Or if I am still asleep,

Or if I care too much.

But the ice cream and Bronze Star and the Commander's words
were all very nice.
Perhaps it is better to be a ghost in the Arabian desert.

The Donkey-Borne Explosive Device

After we found the disabled kid's school cleared out,
And turned into suicide-bombers,
We'd thought we were grizzled.

The bomb-makers moved on to livestock,
In a crowded market,
They strapped a bunch of explosives to a donkey.
They slapped his ass,
And ran him into the middle of a market (Sunni?).

They remote-detonated,
It smelled like bar-b-que.

I feel bad for the donkey.

J.B. STEVENS

Pen Flares

Pen flares are crimson streaks of happiness
in a colorless world.

One-hitter Roman candles.

They are given to young private Soldiers as a deterrent.
Shoot the streak at an approaching bad guy—
A warning (so you don't have to shoot him in the face
with a 5.56 round).

They are good for that,
But young private Soldiers use them for fire-works fights,
Shooting one another,
Or shooting camel-spiders,
Or screwing around.

Pen flares are joyful,
And I saw numerous young men almost light one-another on fire
while laughing and playing in a war zone.
Laughter in a war zone is a precious thing (even if you might light
your battle buddy on fire).

With little red happy veins.

I often think of them and smile.

Outgoing Tracers

I fell asleep to the thump of the Black Hawk's rotors.
And I put my vest under my balls,
And I say my little prayer, every time my little prayer,
    every time the same prayer:
Lord, if I owe you a pound of flesh,
Take my left foot and my left hand,
Not my balls—not my dick,
I want to have a kid,
I need to have a kid,
And don't burn up my face,
I need a woman,
To have a kid,
Take the left side,
They are yours,
I accept the trade.

The door gunner's outgoing shots wake me.

I slept through the incoming.

The sliding door is open and the dry wind is hot and the world is black
    and how is this not a movie?

How is this real life?

I'm from a fucking suburb.

The door gunner returns fire, the outgoing tracers are red.
The incoming tracers are green.

I kept my balls,
And I have a daughter.

J.B. STEVENS

Two Feet

He lost his left foot,
The clutch foot,
And it was a good foot.

He spent all that juicy war-money on a 2006 manual transmission
Dodge Viper.
The Viper was red,
We called him a douchebag,
But I think we were jealous.

I lost nothing,
We were Basic Training company commanders, together,
Eager to leave the schoolhouse,
The training purgatory,
Get to the line,
Lead an infantry platoon, play-act Patton.

Into the shit.

"You want lunch? I'll hit up the Colonel first,"
I ate salami on white bread and took Third Platoon.

Subway's food is not fresh.
He took First.
He lost his clutch foot.
I lost nothing.

Maybe I was jealous.

Developed in 1952 for American Troops

.308 sounds different than,
A pistol,
9-millimeter a fairy's sneeze—metric and European,
.308 a Grizzly's roar.

The main battle rifle, the All-American caliber. Heavy metal.
American exceptionalism in steel and wood and oil and brass
    and smokeless powder and efficient killing.

The 240 I humped in Iraq,
The sniper that gave me sanctified overwatch and murder-on-demand,
Another night, another continent, another bad guy,
But .308 still holds me.

How many forests, how many dusks, how much terror?
Praying I don't catch one.
I try to forget, but the stress takes a piece,
Of me.

Fuck that guy, pointing my caliber at me.

It is mine.

It is so dark, and smells like pine, and why didn't the agency
    buy me night vision?
My kingdom for night vision.
Am I not worth the price of night vision?

The asshole shot a patrolman, with the consecrated .308,
I hope I don't catch one,
But, I know I'm due.

I know I'm due.

When it is time to go, I want to die in a pile of spent and smoking
    and blister-hot brass,
Chasing a bad guy,
With my eyes open and bright and to the face,
Gazing at the .308.

The Mud-Brick Outbuilding

They locked the disabled kid in the barn,
But it is wasn't a true barn,
More a mud-brick outbuilding,
That is how they do it,
I shouldn't hold them to my Western ideals,
Is one culture really better?

We don't lock disabled kids with livestock,
Right?

They are simple farmers, living in mudbrick,
But what the fuck?

He's their kid,
Not a cow.

I have no idea what the right answer is,
The entire fucking thing makes no sense.

Why am I searching a farm outside Baghdad for weapons?
I don't give a shit.

No one cares, it's their country.

It is all so pointless.

I want to go home.

I miss my couch,
And this is all pointless and I don't care.

Am I a mercenary?

My couch is home.

Enduring Freedom

Endure

Iraq took my soul,
Sleep requires medication,
Death beckons peaceful.

Why can't I relax,
The assholes all fucking missed,
I endure.
They missed.

Motivation gone,
My novel consumes the world,
The memories call.

J.B. STEVENS

The Prayer Rug

The knife felt like home,
My cousin made it from my uncle's F-150 leaf spring, he gave it to me before deployment,
I'd never stabbed a man,
It is very red and smells strongly and covers my hand,
But only the left,
The rifle jammed, Arabian dust a puzzle with no solution,
Knives don't jam.

White trash in some city whose name I can't pronounce,
Or remember,
He is the Iraqi version of white trash, I need to learn that word,
A pawn like me, I wish I was dead,
So he dies.

I am not dead,
The prayer rug is covered in blood,
Who is going to feed the cow?

I used to pray I didn't die here,
Death is peace, peace in the now,
I want go back to Georgia,
So he dies.

Knives don't jam.
Arabian dust a puzzle with no solution.

Death is comfort.

Bullet

The bullet comes for me,
I pulled the trigger myself,
Another night of simple pain,
Drown it with Tennessee brown,
I miss my wife,
Swallow the hate.
Why did I choose this shit life?
I chose wrong,
Someone else is in the bed,
My ego is the killer.

J.B. STEVENS

It is Leather

It is black vinyl but I tell you it is leather,
The entire war I missed this couch,
It is odd, loving a thing, missing an object,
Simple comfort, sofa and air-conditioning, home—
When I came back,
She was gone,
The entire world hers to roam.
The new guy doesn't have bad dreams and cry and drink too much.
But what is too much?
The soft embrace was still there.
Security in the familiar.

Training

I did as I was trained,
Why can't I fucking rest?

The movies make it different.

He was the bad guy,
I know—he was the wicked one,
I feel it in my gut.

He shot a pregnant woman in the neck,
And stole an old man's Buick,
A Buick ...

If you are going to murder you should have taste.
Lack of taste is almost unforgivable.

A criminal needs style,

The Drip.

He pointed a Glock at me,
Or was it a cheap knock-off?
The barrel as big as a cave.
A gaping blackhole of terror.

But I wasn't scared,
Idiot doesn't realize I want to die,
And that is good,
Because it makes my life so much more simple,
I don't remember shooting,
But he is dead,
And I earned a medal,
His mom didn't cry on the news,

She just brought a lawsuit,
And she wants money,
And she will get it ... A lot.

Saying her son lost his way and she prayed for him and she tried,
She lit a candle for me,
Because I didn't really have a choice,
I know.

Sleep is a luxury for the innocent.

The First Night

The first night,
I stepped off the Black Hawk,
Chopping the hot dry air,
Roaring loud,
With an electric whine,
Driving sand into my pores.

And Sergeant Silver met me,
Sergeant Silver is my maintenance guru.

And my wise mentor,
Who doesn't know shit about fighting,
But can make anything with an engine run.

He was smoking menthols,
The cherry glowing hot in the dim—until he stepped into the bright.

And wore a short mustache,
He was from Detroit—I think, but I am not sure.

He took me to a large tent,
I dropped my gear on a cot, and went to eat, and a suicide bomber
blew up my tent,
No one was even hurt—except for the bomber,
He wasted his shot, but maybe he got some virgins?

My stuff was gone,
I wasn't,
Death calling scared me.

And Silver laughed.

And, 12 months later, I laughed too.

J.B. STEVENS

Neil

Neil Landsberg killed himself on May 9, 2013.
He hazed me for 9 months in the year 2000—and I appreciate his efforts.

Neil gave me a gift, the blessed kind of suffering,
The kind that make young boys feel like they are not young boys but men of a brotherhood,
Before a war.

And I am forever grateful for Neal.
And The Citadel,
And Alpha Company.

My *alma mater*—a remnant from another time.
The Bastion of Antiquity,
A shining beacon of discipline and hope and the old ways.
Landsberg was more fit,
More confident,
And more competent,
Then anyone I ever knew.

He looked like Captain America,
And when he ran, he glided.
In a world of suffering, he was the king.

He was kind,
After the anguish,
With a twinkle in his eye,
The brotherhood was his goal,
And he achieved it.

He went to the Air Force,
And into Special Operations,

And the war took his calm.

He was the sturdiest of us,
And he killed himself on May 9th, 2013.

And the world cannot forget to remember,
The sturdiest of us.

J.B. STEVENS

LB

LB killed himself with his SAW, somewhere near Baghdad.

I cannot remember what LB stood for.

Something from his last name.

He was fat and white and pasty,
The kind of expendable-poors that joins the Army,
Appalachian and Ghetto and with low S.A.T. scores,
From a town no one heard of or remembers,
The poors are pushed into the Infantry,
And they bleed out in sand.

And redneck guys with something to prove to themselves,
With some college, but no degree,
We are their leaders.

The Squad Automatic Weapon, or M249.
Fires 750 rounds per minute in normal operational mode,
    and 1,000 in maximum.

Is a very mercurial weapon,
And a bitch to clean.

They named our Combat Outpost after him.

But his name was hard to spell,
So it became "COP L.B."

And I can't remember his true name,
And Google brings up nothing,
And we've all forgotten,
And I'm not sure he was even there.

Logan

Logan Lonkard was my gunner,
Before every combat patrol, he would get me an icy Coca-Cola.

And I was his Captain.

He was from Pikeville in the Kentucky hills.

He taught me about the kill-boner (which is real and a natural response
to excitement and not sexual).

Logan kept me safe,
He got very fucked-up in Ramadi,
At the hotel,
But I was at The Citadel that day.

And in Baghdad, Logan kept me alive,
And he made me laugh.
And his angular face and rolling accent made me think of home.
He wanted to be a U.S. Marshal.
But he never crossed that bridge.

He started to drink and went to the V.A.
But that never helps,
But back to Iraqi—we returned to the world,
My driver did cocaine (his name was Lucky).
The fire-team went nuts,
Everyone was chaptered-out,
Abandoned to the American dust and wind and wide-open spaces,
And forgotten.

Because, after enough time, war is far easier than
paying your electric bill,
And triggers will always make more sense than taxes,

And in-country is easy because you only have one problem,
And if you die it is over and that is OK,
Because it is over.

None of us could handle the peace.
I got a nothing job, and I drank for a while,
But I was their Captain,
I have degrees and was never arrested,
So now I have a good job and a mortgage and a wife and a daughter
(the two best people on earth),
Logan died in a single car accident,
On a clear day.

On an empty road.

On a dry road.

On an easy drive.

Thirty-one years old and sharp of mind,
He was going to the VA for a counseling appointment.

He still had a single-car accident.

It is much easier for families to accept,
And insurance payouts to come,
When it is not a suicide,
Or so I've heard.

The Explosion

After the first explosion the checkpoint was fucked.
The Aussie mercenaries rolled up,
They got on our radio.

Three men were dead, but I cannot remember their names,
They were not from my unit,
My platoon Sergeant's leg was also fucked,
I imagine it still is. It was his second purple heart.

I called a MEDEVAC, a 9-Line,
And it is now a T-Shirt company,
I try not to be a whiney bitch, but that is a stupid fucking name.
It is a call of death,
And of suffering,
And pain,
Those wanna-be tough guys wear 9-line T-Shirts because
　　they hate Obama,
Or something.

The Aussies gave morphine and pulled security,
And I got a MEDEVAC bird up,
And three people died—but that was not my fault (I think),
I did my best (I think),
I did all I could (I think),
The Aussies were cool, but three people died, and that leg was fucked.

And I cannot remember any names.

Aftershocks

The VBIED's Aftershock

When the Checkpoint blew up,
It shook my guts and chewed my soul,
And I took the next shift in the Bradley with the good vision and the big gun and the twenty-five-mike-mike Bushmaster cannon.
Ready to rock someone's shit.

We set a serpentine,
With Arabic writing:
Don't Drive Past Here
PAIN IS HERE
You Will Die
Death Calls

But that Iraqi in the shitty white car still drove through,
So, I shot him in the chin (through the windshield),
He stopped,
And opened a door and rolled out of the car.

It blew out the left side of his face, at the muscle where you chew.
My interpreter was an Assyrian Christian and Baghdad native that lost everything when he ran to California and he told me to shoot the driver,
But my interpreter always told me to shoot everyone as he chain-smoked,
He hated Muslims and wanted me to commit war-crimes to punish the perceived source of his pain,
The interpreter kept asking me for a gun,
And he loved war-crimes,
But I never did.

I don't like to shoot people.

I didn't want to commit war-crimes—so I never did.

The driver, with the now-missing face muscles, was very drunk,
And he probably couldn't read, so the drive-through was an accident.

He cried and apologized.
I called the Iraqi police.

And I never learned what happened,
And I don't know if I killed him,
Or just shot him in the face.

Specialist Wiens and Cooper the Dog

Wiens and Cooper were my handler and bomb-dog combo.
I remember their names.
Bomb dogs are special,
Cooper, yellow and silky and kind, was the most special.

If a dog isn't trained in apprehension,
And is yellow and silky and kind,
They are like a happy pet,
And their life is a game,
War zone be dammed.

If they find the scent, they get a treat and they are joyful.
But the scent is explosives—so maybe that is dangerous.
Cooper never found shit,
And I loved him with all my soul.

And one day I left Iraq, but Cooper and Wiens were not in my unit,
so they stayed,
After I was home Cooper found a cache of something,
I don't know what, because I wasn't there, and I read about it on
WikiLeaks,
(All my really bad days are on WikiLeaks.)

Cooper was blown to fuck,
Wiens stood by Cooper's side.

They are gone,
And I hope it didn't hurt,
But, at least, they were together,
But, at least, I remember their names.

J.B. STEVENS

War is Great

After the war,
I became a cop, or something close to that.

War is great because it is clear, if you are in the Infantry,
    and you are on the line—
You shoot the bad guy,
Or he shoots you,
And that is your day,
And it is violent, but simple and clear and righteous
    (when you are twenty-two years old),
The clarity is healing and pure and I often miss it.

For the cop, or something close to that, it is never clear.
It is murk and confusion and so much more pain.
The first warrant was a meth dealer who made masturbation videos of
    himself while smoking crystal and wearing a *Scream* movie mask.

It was a Thursday night.
How do I explain that to my wife when she asks how my day was?
I can't.

Sometimes she thinks I'm closed-off,
But I'm not,
I just miss war.

In war, everything makes so much sense.
And it is great.

I Left the Wire

The first time I left the wire,
Visions of *Saving Private Ryan* danced in my head.

We saw things,
But didn't shoot,
And we came back to the outpost,
And I shook with the excitement of it all,
And I read Hemingway (because I was a young white man in a war
    and that is what a young warrior white man must do).

But it was over.
The first patrol was short,
The first patrol was a letdown.

And it will forever feel unfinished.

J.B. STEVENS

The Bunker

One time I was watching a Stephen King movie called *1408*,
But if I tell you this story at a writing conference, I will say I was reading the book,
And if you meet me there, and you've read this line, tell no one of my secret,
It can be your secret as well.

And it can be a special private thing that we share,
And I can wink at you.
You and I are now bonded.

Tell no one.

And while I was watching *1408*, I was in a shitty tin-can-trailer,
South of Baghdad,
The incoming rockets came, a propane tank on a propellant—terribly loud.

But I didn't care,
Because they always came,
And I think maybe I wanted to die,
Or I was just tired of living,
An apathetic existence,
A life in sepia,
However, when that first rocket hit, the movie had a jump-scare,
Mr. King made a grab for John Cusack (a sweetheart of an actor).

And I ran to a bunker shaking.
My Sergeant was there, and he couldn't understand my tremors,
Because he knew of the apathy,
His give-fuck-reserves were even lower than mine.
I told him I was watching a horror move,
Alone,

At night,
In a war zone.

He called me a "Fucking Retard" and now I know that is offensive
    and can get a writer canceled and it is just plain morally wrong—
    but in 2008 in a war I didn't know these things so I said nothing.

This is another secret you and I can share.
But it was very stupid, to watch a movie like that alone in a war zone,
    and I do not even like scary movies,
    and I do not even write horror stories.

And now you know the clandestine truth,
And you and I can wink at one another at a conference
    and share a secret,
Or something.

J.B. STEVENS

The Palm Grove

One time I was shot at,
From a palm grove.
It was green but covered in dust, as these things are.

I was inside an armored vehicle,
So, the shooter was very fucking stupid.

The helicopters flew over,
And they told me it was a village,
And they told me the terrorists were intermingled,
But they wouldn't stop shooting at me,
So, I shot back,

And it was painful,
And I don't know what happened after I returned fire,
Because I don't want to know,
I never looked,
I never can,
And I never will.

But the shooting stopped.

When I First Returned

My fiancée cheated on me when I was in-country for 90 days.
This was very fortunate,
Because she was a fiancée and not a wife, and didn't have access to my finances,
A wife would have.

So, I had a broken heart,
And a damaged soul,
And a full bank-account.

I returned and was lost and took a trip to Prague.
It is a beautiful city,
But I kept waking up screaming.

I was traveling with my fire-support officer,
3-0.

3-0 was with me the whole war, and he understood,
So, he never said anything. And when I see him at things, he doesn't talk about that, and I am thankful for his discretion.

And eventually the screaming stopped.
And Prague is still a gorgeous city,
And the money was used well.

A Short War Story

A Wartime Breakfast with Ramirez

Bonus Short Fiction by J.B. Stevens

An explosion jarred me, and I opened my eyes and knew exactly where I was and there was no confusion. In the beginning of my wartime, when someone tried to shoot me or blow me up, it was disconcerting. After a while it became a part of life, and I almost forgot it was not a normal thing to be almost blown-up, but I'd stopped caring. My feelings had stopped working.

I didn't like that they'd left, and I tried to fix it, but nothing had yet worked.

I jumped out of bed, grabbed my M4, put on my dollar-store flip-flops, and ran to my grey-concrete bunker. Mine.

Ramirez was already there. He had a deck of cards. While everything blew up we played five-card-draw poker—no betting. It is less fun without gambling but much cheaper. I usually lose, so this was a best-case scenario.

I pulled out my Skoal wintergreen chewing tobacco and filled the space between my lip and gums with the black shredded leaves.

Ramirez gave me shit about the wintergreen again. I told him to stop, but he kept up. The minty smell mixed with the grey dust air. Airborne grit got in my nose and the back of my throat. It made my eyes water.

We talked about women, and Ramirez gave me hell about not having a woman back home. I didn't tell him about the tattoo-face girl I met on the last patrol outside the wire. Soldiers and locals didn't mix, and he wouldn't understand. But my existence was redundant, and I didn't care, and she made it less so.

The enemy fire kept oozing in. Soon, I heard our artillery's outgoing shots. After thirty minutes of back-and-forth indirect death-tag, it was over as if it never started and never happened.

When it was done, Ramirez grinned at me. "Breakfast?"

"Yeah." I said. "Let me get dressed."

We went to my housing unit. Ramirez held my rifle and waited outside. Inside, I put on my uniform. My boots fit tighter than normal, and I wondered why. I exited and we went to the chow hall.

The building had been hit by incoming, and there was a hole in the north-side corner roof and the north wall. I was glad the hole was far from the hot-chow line, that way no dirt got in my food.

I grabbed a brown plastic tray and got in line. Quickly, I got to the front. A Bangladeshi food-service contractor gave me scrambled eggs, bacon, pork sausage, a bagel with cream cheese, and pancakes. The food looked great, and I was excited and thankful.

I got a cup of black coffee and a glass of orange juice. The food reminded me of Waffle House back home—I'd gone there often with my father and loved the place. I sat down in a blue plastic chair that reminded me of grade school. Ramirez, sat across from me; he had just had bacon and eggs.

I pointed at his plate. "What's up?"

Ramirez slapped his not-huge-but-noticeable belly. "Going keto."

"Yeah? Why?"

"I got to look good when I get home." He laughed. "Keep the wife from cheating on me."

I laughed. "*More*—cheating on you *more*."

Ramirez stopped rubbing his belly. "What do you mean?"

"You know she's getting pounded by some fireman right now."

Ramirez frowned and forced a chuckle. The two Air Force sergeants sitting next to us laughed too loud and guilt bubbled in my gut.

"I'm just playing," I said. "I'm sure she can't wait for you to get home and isn't running around or nothing."

Ramirez winked. "Of course, no worries." He looked down and ate his eggs.

My guilt metastasized.

I held up my full coffee cup. "I'm going to get more. Can I get you something?"

"No, I'm good," Ramirez said. "Thanks."

His voice seemed more alive and that made me glad. I didn't want to hurt my friends. I didn't want to hurt anyone.

I walked to the shiny stainless-steel coffee percolator. It was always perfect-looking, and I wondered if some Bangladeshi guy spent every night cleaning the thing. A guy moves across the world to work for the mighty American war effort and spends his days wiping fingerprints off a hunk of metal that does nothing other than pour hot water over crushed beans.

I was a touch jealous, because that seemed like a good and simple and honest existence—maintain a thing that provides happiness to others. Simple and clean and righteous and no moral grey.

Everything I did, every day ... did it make anyone happy? Did my bullshit make anyone's life better? Maybe being the coffee guy is more important than being whatever the hell I was.

Since my coffee cup was full, the quest being a ruse, I poured the dark liquid in a trash can. I refilled my cup. The scent was strong and good. I loved that smell in the morning. I took a sip, and it was too hot but tasted great. The food and services were always top-shelf at the base, and I appreciated it. I walked to the line and found a Bangladeshi food-service worker.

I made eye contact with the man. "Thank you," I said as I raised my coffee cup.

The worker, who was short and dark-haired, with grey skin, waved and smiled. He was missing a front tooth, and the other was light green. His grin appeared genuine, and I wondered if he was the coffee percolator operator. I wanted to dig into the mystery, but Ramirez hooted so I walked back to the table.

Ramirez's eggs and bacon were gone, as was my bagel.

"I thought you were eating keto," I asked.

Ramirez shrugged. "Every diet needs a cheat day."

"How long you been on the diet?"

"This is my first day," Ramirez said. "Figure I get the cheating out of the way now and it is all smooth sailing."

"Smart."

"If you're gonna be dumb, you gotta be tough."

"I've heard."

"And I'm not tough."

"So you're smart?"

Ramirez tapped his temple with his right index finger. "They're playing checkers and I'm playing chess."

I laughed.

Ramirez pointed left. "That lady came looking for you."

I looked. Bassinette Reeves stood in the corner by the wall-hole.

Light from the roof-hole shot down on her like a laser through the dust.

She sipped coffee, and I thought of the phantom percolator operator. I stood up and walked over.

She shook my hand and held up her coffee. "You had any of this?" I felt warm inside, another percolator appreciator. "Yeah." She turned and threw the cup in the trash. "That's shitty coffee." My throat got tight. "Sure." Wind rushed through the mortar-hole in the wall, and I hoped she would leave soon. "What can I do for you?" She gestured to an empty table. We walked over and sat.

"I wanted to let you know," Reeves said. "Our investigation into Sergeant Golds' death is complete."

"And?"

She sighed. "It was a freak accident that occurred because he was raising drugged-up fighting scorpions."

"Seriously?"

"Yeah. We even brought in an arachnologist from the Smithsonian."

"What's that?"

"The Smithsonian?"

I frowned. "I'm not an idiot; what's an arachnologist?"

"A person with a Ph.D. in bugs. In this case, a specializing in scorpions."

"You brought an insect professor to a war zone?"

"We brought the doctor to Germany—we sent the body to an Air Force base there."

"I guess that makes more sense?"

"The arachnologist did a bunch of tests along with a coroner."

"And?"

"Golds was stung hundreds of times—it overwhelmed his system and he died." A tear crept out of the corner of Reeves's eye.

"It had nothing to do with the scorpion fights or gambling a money or any of that?"

Reeves looked at him cross-eyed. "You think you're in a John Le Carré novel?"

"No," I said. "Why?"

"There's not always some grand design. It's a fucking war."

"So?"

"So people die for stupid reasons, and it is done." More tears came. Reeves stood. "It's a fucking war?"

I looked at the lines cutting down her face. "Did you know Golds?"

"I did. We both got here a year ago. I know him ... well." Reeves turned and walked away. She left through the chow-hall's door—even though the explosion hole was right there and leaving through an explosion hole is a once-in-a-lifetime opportunity.

I thought about the tattoo-face girl from the last mission outside the wire and wondered if she was OK, and everything was bit a bit better after thinking of her.

I walked back to the percolator, got another cup, and returned to my table. Ramirez had eaten my pancake and left, so my breakfast was over.

I exited the building through the bomb-hole and went back to my housing: I thought of Reeves' tears and the girl with the blue tattoo lines on her face.

I felt something.

Acknowledgements

"As I Clean My Rifle" first appeared at *The Line Literary Review*, Fall 2021

"Endure" first appeared in *Punk Noir Magazine*, Sept. 24, 2020

"The Explosion" first appeared in *The Deadly Writers Patrol* No. 18, Spring 2021 under the title "Dead—Not from My Unit"

"Fat Cook Gunfight" first appeared in *Punk Noir Magazine*, Oct. 25, 2020

"A Ghost in an Arabian Desert" first appeared in *Punk Noir Magazine*, Dec. 12, 2020

"The Iraqi Female Suicide Bomber Who Blew Off Her Arms and Legs," first appeared in *Line of Advance* literary journal in August 2021, where it won second-place in that year's Col. Darron L. Wright Memorial Writing Awards.

"Specialist Wiens and Cooper the Dog" first appeared in *The Deadly Writers Patrol* No. 18, Spring 2021

"This French 75" first appeared at *Rock and a Hard Place Press Magazine*, No. 5, Winter/Spring Mar. 11, 2021

"The VBIED's Aftershock" first appeared in *The Deadly Writers Patrol* No. 18, Spring 2021 under the title "The Dump Truck Bomb's Aftershock"

"A Wartime Breakfast with Ramierez" first appeared in *Proud to Be: Writing by American Warriors, Vol. 10*, Southeast Missouri State University Press, 2022

Glossary

5.56 ("Five-point-Five-Six"; sometimes "Five-Five-Six"): The NATO standard caliber for rifle ammunition is 5.56mm.

Black Hawk: The UH-60 "Black Hawk" utility helicopter is a four-blade, twin-engine, medium-lift manufactured by Sikorsky Aircraft. It can transport up to 11 troops with equipment.

Bronze Star Medal (B.S.M.): The Bronze Star Medal is awarded to members of the United States Armed Forces for either heroic achievement or service (indicated by a "V" pin on the medal), meritorious achievement, or meritorious service in a combat zone.

C.A.B. (sometimes pronounced "Kab"): First issued in 2005, the U.S. Army Combat Action Badge is awarded to non-Infantry personnel for being "present and actively engaged by the enemy" at any time after Sept. 11, 2001.

C.I.B.: First issued in 1943, the U.S. Army "Combat Infantryman Badge" is awarded to Infantry- and Special Forces-branch who participate in active ground combat. Non-Infantry soldiers are eligible for the Combat Action Badge.

C.L.P. ("Cleaner, Lubricant, Preservative"): A type of a liquid issued to U.S. military personnel for maintaining small arms, such as rifles and pistols. Sometimes called "Break-Free," which is a registered trademark.

COP (pronounced "Kahp"): "Combat Outpost." A small, fortified location from which U.S. military forces can defend and perform limited resupply.

E.F.P. ("Explosively Formed Penetrator"; sometimes also "Explosively Formed Projectile"): A type of shaped-charge designed to, upon detonation, form a projectile that will penetrate armored vehicles.

Some types of Improvised Explosive Devices feature specially machined solid-copper discs, which serve this function.

F-150 (pronounced "EFF-one-fifty"): A model of light-duty truck manufactured by the Ford Motor Co.

French 75: A cocktail made from gin, champagne, lemon juice, and sugars. Invented in 1915 in Paris by barman Harry MacElhone, the effect was described as having a kick similar to that of a French 75mm field artillery piece.

Glock: A family of semi-automatic pistols manufactured by Austrian company Glock Ges.m.b.H. The pistols feature a combination of metal and polymer components.

I.E.D.: Improvised Explosive Device. A "homemade" bomb or mine constructed of parts, including military scrap or surplus, not originally intended for such use.

M240 (pronounced "EM-two-forty"): A standard, belt-fed medium machine-gun used by U.S. military forces. Fires a 7.62mm round.

M4 ("EM-four"): A shortened, "carbine" variant of the M16 family of assault rifles used by U.S. military forces. Fires a 5.56mm round. Carbines are easier to use in close-quarters, and to carry in vehicles.

MEDEVAC ("MED-evak"): "Medical Evacuation"

"9-Line": A standardized U.S. military report format for requesting MEDEVAC over a tactical radio net. To help reduce response times, troops practice train to make these requests efficient and brief.

M.F.A. "Master of Fine Arts." A type of graduate-level academic degree, often focused on creative writing.

M16 (pronounced "EM-six-teen"): The family of semi-automatic assault rifles issued to U.S. Army soldiers since 1969. It fires a 5.56mm round, usually as either single shots or three-round "bursts." The M4 carbine gradually replaced the M16 rifle starting in 1994.

M203 (pronounced "EM-too-oh-three"): A single-shot 40mm grenade launcher that mounts under the barrel of an M16 rifle or M4 carbine. Grenadiers are trained to engage targets by up to 350 meters away.

P.T.S.D.: Post-Traumatic Stress Disorder. A medical condition stemming from exposures to actual or threatened death, serious injury, or sexual violence—including exposures through the experiences of others—that result in persistent negative alterations of an individual's thinking, emotions, sleep, and other behaviors. More fully and formally described in the American Psychological Association's *Diagnostic and Statistical Manual of Mental Disorders (DSM).*

S.A.T.: Founded in 1926 as the Scholastic Aptitude Test, the assessment test taken by U.S. high-school juniors and seniors is now called the SAT.

"SAW". The U.S. "Squad Automatic Weapon" M249 is a light, usually belt-fed, fully automatic machine gun. Fires a 5.56mm round. Bridges the gap in capabilities between the M4/M16 assault rifle and the M240B heavy machine gun.

.308 ("Three-Oh-Eight"): The .308 Winchester is a bullet of similar caliber and design to the cartridge known as "30-caliber" or 7.62mm.

WikiLeaks: A Sweden-based non-profit organization that publicly publishes secret information submitted by anonymous sources. The organization was founded in 2006 by Australian citizen Julian Assange.

V.A.: The U.S. Department of Veterans Affairs

VBEID ("VEE-bid"): "Vehicle-Borne Improvised Explosive Device."

A Few Words of Thanks

Erica and Claire, you are my heart.

To the Citadel class of '04 (and especially "A" Company)—I'm glad we were there together.

To the other "A" Company mates—those that didn't make it—I remember you.

To Logan, this Silver Star is half yours.

To Dr. Saylor, you had more of an influence than you will ever know.

Doug, Jason, and Steve—thanks.

About the Author

Iraq War veteran J.B. Stevens is a writer of fiction, non-fiction, and poetry, often delivering hardboiled action, gritty conflict, and dark humor. His collection of noirish short-fiction, *A Therapeutic Death: Violent Short Stories,* was published in 2022 by Shotgun Honey Books. Infused with TV and other pop-culture references, Stevens' debut poetry collection, *The Best of America Cannot Be Seen: Pop Poems,* was published in 2021 by Alien Buddha Press.

Stevens is a contributing editor for *Mystery Tribune Magazine*, a publication that covers and publishes mystery, suspense, and crime genres. He is also a reviewer and interviewer for *Criminal Element*, an on-line journal published by St. Martin's Press.

Stevens was a 2019 finalist for the Claymore Award, which is administered by the Killer Nashville International Writers' Conference. He was also a 2022 finalist for the Terry Kay Prize administered by the Atlanta Writers Club, and the winner of *Mystery Tribune* inaugural micro-fiction contest in Summer 2019.

Stevens is a two-time past finalist in the Col. Darron L. Wright Memorial Writing Awards, with one award each in prose (2022) and poetry (2021) categories. The annual awards are administered by the Chicago-based literary journal *Line of Advance.*

Before launching his writing career, Stevens was an infantry officer in the U.S. Army. He was awarded a Bronze Star Medal for his wartime service in Iraq. He is also an undefeated Mixed Martial Arts Fighter and a Black Belt in Brazilian Jiujitsu. He graduated from The Citadel, a military college in Charleston, South Carolina. He lives in the Southeastern United States with his wife and daughter.

❖ ❖ ❖

A three-story collection of "fast-paced, exciting, and fun crime stories," *This Will Not End Well: Deadly Stories,* is available *free* via the author's website.

Visit: **www.jb-stevens.com**

Also from Middle West Press

anthology

Our Best War Stories: Prize-winning Poetry & Prose from the Col. Darron L. Wright Memorial Awards
Edited by Christopher Lyke

❖ ❖ ❖

poetry collections

Unwound: Poems from Enduring Wars
by Liam Corley

The Time War Takes
by Jessi M. Atherton

Hugging This Rock: Poems of Earth & Sky, Love & War
by Eric Chandler

Permanent Change of Station and *FORCES*
by Lisa Stice

Always Ready: Poems from a Life in the U.S. Coast Guard
by Benjamin B. White

September Eleventh: an epic poem, in fragments
by Amalie Flynn

Blood / Not Blood ... Then the Gates
by Ron Riekki

HEAT + PRESSURE: Poems from War
by Ben Weakley

Made in the USA
Monee, IL
09 September 2023

42429573R00049